HOPI

FOLLOWING THE PATH OF PEACE

NATIVE AMERICAN WISDOM

CHRONICLE BOOKS

SAN FRANCISCO

A Labyrinth Book

First published in the United States in 1994 by Chronicle Books.

Copyright © 1994 by Labyrinth Publishing (UK) Ltd.

Design by Meringue Management

The Little Wisdom Library–Native American Wisdom was produced by Labyrinth Publishing (UK) Ltd. Printed and bound in Singapore by Craft Print Pte. Ltd.

Library of Congress Cataloging in Publication Data: Hopi, Native American Wisdom.

p.   cm. (Native American Wisdom) Includes bibliographical references.

ISBN 0–8118–0430–5

1. Hopi Indians —Folklore. 2. Hopi Indians—Social life and customs.

3. Hopi Indians—Philosophy. I. Chronicle Books (Firm) II. Series.

E99. H7H67   1994

398.2'. 089' 074– dc20   92–41821

                                                                        CIP

Distributed in Canada by Raincoast Books,

112 East Third Avenue, Vancouver, B.C. V5T 1C8

10 9 8 7 6 5 4 3 2 1

Chronicle Books

275 Fifth Street, San Francisco, CA 94103

Introduction

The Western world breaks life into separate compartments, as clearly divided as the borders of Great Plains states, in an attempt to understand the secrets of the universe. Native America views humans and their surroundings as interconnected within a sacred circle. It holds the essences of being and becoming. One of the ironies of American history is the containment of the Hopi, the oldest carriers of ancient Indian beliefs and practices, inside a rectilinear reservation. Yet on the remote, high Hopi mesas life can still be followed in natural curving contours, physical and metaphysical.

The Hopi pay in work and sweat for their relative solitude. Theirs is a desert country with no secure water sources on the mesas where they have located their villages. The men have to descend about six hundred feet along steep narrow paths to the flatlands

below. Once there, further travel is necessary to reach the plots of land assigned them by village chiefs to grow the corn, beans, and squash to sustain life. As late as the 1890s, ninety percent of the tribe's vegetable diet was corn— yellow, red, black, and blue. They still nurture the seeds as in past eras, locating the areas of maximum drainage around the heads of arroyos or along the region's few streams, sometimes irrigating from springs.

An entire day can be used up in going to the field, cultivating, and returning up the mesa walls. Visitors look at the minuscule patches of growing corn incredulously—a few scraggly plants, often no more than three feet high at maximum growth. What they do

not see is the fifteen to twenty feet of root system straining for moisture caught and trapped where tradition informs the Hopi to plant their seeds. It seems a strange sort of farming to the uninitiated, but it represents a successful blending of the Hopi world: Mother Earth and rain. In common with other American Indians, the Hopi understand and accept the holistic

Previous page 4: This carved and painted doll represents a deity in the Hopi pantheon known as Calako. The head ornament signifies rain clouds. *Previous page 7:* The Flute Ceremony takes place in alternating years in mid-August. It brings late summer rains, ensures a successful harvest, and re-enacts the emergence into the Fourth World.
Previous pages 8-9: These abandoned cave dwellings in New Mexico were probably occupied by Hopi clans early in their cycle of migrations. *Opposite:* Kachinas such as these painted by Hopi artist Kabotie are spirits from the other world who visit the Hopis during the growing season.

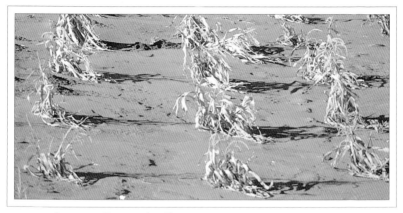

aspect of nature. Desert dwellers, they have fashioned their rich ceremonial existence around the most significant phenomenon of their cognizance, water from the sky fertilizing the land to sustain life.

Ritual guides the Hopi cycle of being. The tribespeople believe

Above: A Hopi cornfield after the harvest. Roots of Hopi corn, unlike other varieties, grow deep into the earth to get enough moisture to survive in the desert environment.

that deities from another world determine much of what occurs in their dimension. During part of the year, until winter solstice, these powerful beings called kachinas dwell in their own land. Then they visit the Hopis, inhabit the bodies of men for a time, and bring rain, laughter, terror, and teaching. They possess awesome powers, and they number in the hundreds, so that Hopi parents make wooden dolls to represent the various kachinas, giving them to their children to study and ponder in preparation for adult participation in kachina dances.

In the deepest, long course of the life of the Hopi it matters little if outsiders seeking the exotic have collected these dolls, serious tools for instruction, and decorate museums and dwellings with them. It matters little if tourists and social scientists invade the ceremonial dances that bring rain, trying to photograph that which is not meant for the purpose of filling blanks in vacation albums and academic texts. It matters little if the federal government has interfered with the internal governance of the villages and allowed the exploitation of Hopi lands for coal to quell a nation's energy appetites. It matters little because of the truth known by even the Navajo, close neighbors but often in conflict with the people of the mesas—only the Hopi can dance and summon the life-giving rain.

Terry P. Wilson
Professor of Native American Studies
University of California, Berkeley

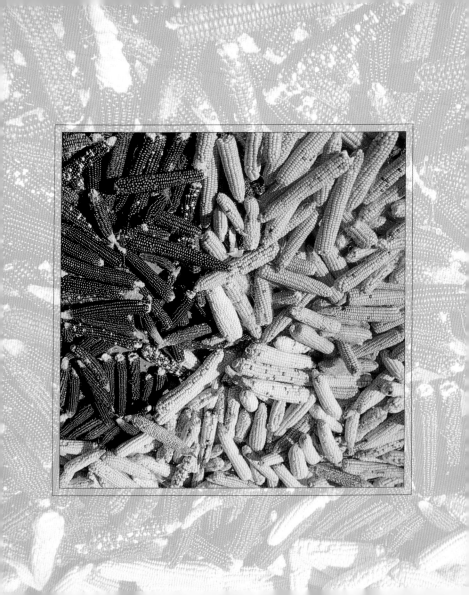

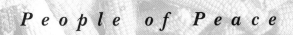

People of Peace

An old Hopi teaching story, often told today, tells of a gathering of all the Native American peoples just after they had emerged into this world. Spread before them was a variety of corn, of all colors and sizes, and their task was to choose for themselves one variety to sustain them on their journeys through life. The other tribes all grabbed the largest, most succulent varieties, while the Hopi representative just waited. Finally only one ear of corn was left, which was small and dark. But the Hopis were satisfied. Some say that this corn was the same variety they had known in the First World, at the beginning of time. They knew its deep, spreading roots would enable it to thrive and grow in the harshest climates.

Whatever the case, those who tell the story today say that this small, dark corn symbolized the fact that even though they would have to work hard, they would live long, full lives.

Previous page: Varieties of corn grown by Hopis today. *Above:* The mask of the Kachina Chackwaina, "One Who Cries."

Albert Yava, a Tewa whose father was a Hopi and who was initiated into a Hopi kiva society, recalls the significance of this narrative in his memoirs:

All through their migrations after that, there were prophecies that the Hopis would make their final home at an austere place where life would be difficult. But their guiding spirit promised to watch over them if they led decent lives. The Hopis were not supposed to accumulate wealth, but to be generous with everything. And when they settled here in this country they said, "Life will be hard in this place, but no one will envy us. No one will try to take our land away. This is the place we will stay."

The word Hopi means "peace," and this story of the corn, along with countless other stories composing their rich oral tradition, illustrates the humble acceptance of their Creator's plan that is central to the Hopi way of life. They travel a "Road of Life" that grows ever more arduous, and where every hardship is seen as a challenge to remember their spiritual heritage and adhere to its teachings. Their survival depends on this remembrance, and their ability to bring rain to the desert and earn their living in this unforgiving place is their proof that they are in accordance with the teachings. Their death, if they have lived rightly, is but another step, a voyage into other worlds, where their travels on the great Road of Life will continue.

The Creation

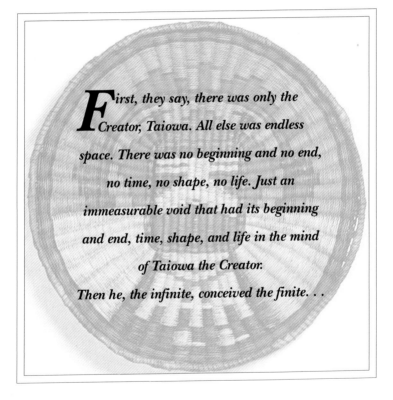

First, they say, there was only the Creator, Taiowa. All else was endless space. There was no beginning and no end, no time, no shape, no life. Just an immeasurable void that had its beginning and end, time, shape, and life in the mind of Taiowa the Creator.
Then he, the infinite, conceived the finite...

Thus begins the extraordinary Hopi story of the Creation. It is extraordinary because this story, and the teachings that flow from it, represent what is certainly the oldest and most comprehensive existing oral history of the native peoples of North America. Extraordinary because these stories reveal tantalizing clues to the origins of the Hopis and their connections to native peoples throughout the Western Hemisphere. Extraordinary because they hint at an advanced understanding of the laws of nature that our contemporary civilization believes it has "discovered" only in the past couple of centuries. And also extraordinary because of the resonance between the Hopi spiritual teachings and many of the ancient teachings of the East.

The Hopi Creator, Taiowa, is not the "father" of Judeo-Christian theology but an "uncle" whose first creation was a nephew, Sotuknang. To Sotuknang he gave the task of manifesting the finite out of the infinite, of transforming vision into reality. This Sotuknang did, creating nine universal kingdoms: one for Taiowa, one for himself, and seven universes for the life that was to come. Each of these

Previous page and background opposite: A basket plaque of the type used in Hopi ceremonials depicts the Sun deity.

universes was composed half of solid and half of water, and surrounded by airs arranged into "gentle, ordered movements." To these three elements, earth, water, and air, Taiowa then instructed Sotuknang to add the fourth and final element, that of life and its movement.

Spider Woman and the Creation of Life

To carry out his task of creating life, Sotuknang went to the First World, the universe named Tokpela, and created a woman to help him. Her name was Kokyangwuti, or Spider Woman.

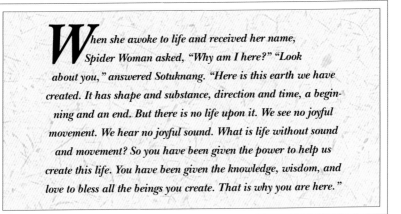

When she awoke to life and received her name, Spider Woman asked, "Why am I here?" "Look about you," answered Sotuknang. "Here is this earth we have created. It has shape and substance, direction and time, a beginning and an end. But there is no life upon it. We see no joyful movement. We hear no joyful sound. What is life without sound and movement? So you have been given the power to help us create this life. You have been given the knowledge, wisdom, and love to bless all the beings you create. That is why you are here."

Contained in the story of Spider Woman's creation of life is evidence that the Hopis have long understood that the earth is not flat but round, rotating on an axis with poles north and south. This function was kept in order by twin beings who were created by Spider Woman, each of whom was given a separate task before taking up his station at one of the poles. One twin traveled the earth forming the solid matter into mountains and fields; the other was told to fill the world with sound.

The traditional description of this latter twin's achievements is beautifully poetic. But it can also be seen as a stunning allegory for ancient understanding of electromagnetic forces that were unknown to European scientists prior to the middle of the nineteenth century. The story says: "All the vibratory centers along the earth's axis from pole to pole resounded his call; the whole earth trembled; the universe quivered in tune. Thus he made the whole world an instrument of sound, and sound an instrument for carrying messages, resounding praise to the Creator of all." Students of Eastern philosophy have noted the importance of sound in this Hopi view of the Creation, and its correspondence to the significance of the syllable "om" or "aum" in the Tibetan tradition. The Tibetans speak of a divine, "soundless sound" representing the creation, preservation, and transformation of the universe.

The Creation of Mankind

As in the creation accounts of many cultures, the human being was the last life form to be created on the earth. But the Hopi account of Creation displays no trace of the ethnocentric viewpoint common to so many other traditions. The first people were created by Spider Woman in all the four colors of black, red, white, and yellow.

Each of the four races was given a different language to speak, and the "pristine wisdom" to understand that the earth was not to be dominated and conquered but was, rather, their mother. The corn that sustained them, because it became part of their flesh, was the earthly manifestation of their mother. The sun, who gave life to the whole universe and served as the "face" of the Creator Taiowa, was perceived as their father. And these two, earth and sun together, were their real parents. The human parents of a child were just the vehicles through whom the power of these spiritual parents could be expressed.

The First World of Tokpela

The world inhabited by these first people created by Spider Woman was one where they lived together in harmony with nature and all her creatures. They were also in

---

Opposite: The small clay bell held by this kachina represents the "vibratory centers" of the earth, and is an important part of the Wuwuchim ceremonial celebrating the dawn of Creation.

---

harmony with all their fellow human beings, and understood one another despite their differences of color and language.

Inhabitants of the First World followed an elaborate set of guidelines to introduce each new child into the world when he or she was born, and forms of these rituals are followed by many Hopi clans today. At the age of seven or eight, when they were old enough to understand, the spiritual instruction of children would begin. The purpose of the instruction was to make the children aware that, in addition to belonging to their earthly family and clan, they were the children of the universe. As their capacity for understanding grew, they would identify themselves more and more with this concept of universal citizenship.

One of the most intriguing elements of the Hopi descriptions of the First World lies in their portrayal of the spiritual nature of man. They refer to energy centers which correspond to different aspects of man's spiritual development, and where "disorders" of the spirit manifest themselves. Students of Eastern mysticism and medicine will note a correspondence to the system of "chakras" and to the systems underlying acupuncture. The unique contribution of the Hopis to this ancient wisdom is in its explicit acknowledgment of the unity of the human body with the body of the earth that sustains and nourishes it.

The living body of man and the living body of the earth are constructed in the same way. Through each runs an axis, man's axis being the backbone, the vertebral column, which controls the equilibrium of his movements and his functions. Along this axis are several vibratory centers that echo the primordial sound of life throughout the universe, or sound a warning if anything goes wrong.

These vibratory centers are used in the Hopi tradition both in diagnosing and treating illnesses. As in the Eastern system of chakras ultimate importance is given to the center at the top of the head, the "first vibratory center," or the "open door" through which a person receives his or her life and communicates with the Creator. This center, just as it is in the Eastern view, is also the place from which the spirit departs the body at death.

Right: Watercolor painting by Edwin Earle, c. 1935. This painting depicts one of the kachina dancers who takes part in the Powamu ceremonial at the beginning of spring. Powamu is traditionally the time that children are initiated either into the Powamu or Kachina Society. Initiations take place just every four years, and children are given a bow or a rattle in preparation for the ceremony.

The Hopi Road
of Life

The Road of Life of the Hopis in its largest sense is represented as a journey through all the seven universes created at the beginning by Taiowa's nephew Sotuknang. At death, the conduct of a person in accordance with the Creator's plan determines where and when the next step on the road will be taken.

To explain the entire system in all its mysterious and profound detail is not possible in this small book, and would be difficult in any case. Early accounts by white observers of the Hopis are seriously flawed by the prejudices and misunderstandings of their times. It is possible that much of the esoteric tradition has been lost in this century, and it is certain that much of it is still held secret by the elders of the Hopi clans. Often, apparently, it is purposely misstated in an understandable reluctance to hand out freely that which is meant to be known only by initiates who are profoundly committed to a spiritual way of life.

But it is safe to say that the Hopi understanding of the plan of the Creator is reflected in all their ceremonies and encompasses all aspects of life,

from the birth and death of the individual to the everyday movements of the sun and stars, from the yearly cycle of the seasons to the birth and destruction of worlds. The Hopi ceremonials are both an aid in remembering this plan and an essential force in its unfoldment. Each of the Hopi clans has its unique role to play, and each role is an essential part of the whole. In the final analysis it is not individual heroism or accomplishments that are important, although certainly each individual has a responsibility to live his or her life in accordance with the plan. But the essential thing is the plan itself,

and to carry it out means that the Hopis must live in harmony with one another, with nature, and with the plan. Out of this complex interplay, then, the plan is both created and allowed to unfold.

The Journey to Tuwaqachi

The First World of the Hopis was corrupted not so much by evil as by "forgetting." The people had been instructed by Sotuknang and Spider Woman to respect their Creator, and to use their vibratory centers to help them

follow his plan. But as they began to forget this, they began to quarrel among themselves. Finally, the situation reached a point where Sotuknang and Taiowa decided that the world had to be destroyed.

Sotuknang appeared before those "chosen people" who still remembered the Creator and his plan, and told them that the doors at the tops of their heads would lead them to safety before he destroyed the world. They followed his indication, and took refuge underground with the Ant People as the First World was destroyed by fire, and a Second World was created for their emergence.

The Second World was almost as beautiful as the first, with the significant difference that the animals no longer trusted humans and remained separate from them. But here, too, people began to forget the plan of the Creator, until finally this world also had to be destroyed.

Previous pages 30-31: These "racing kachinas" portrayed by the Hopi artist Kabotie traditionally enter foot races with children, purposely losing so the children can be presented with small gifts. *Above:* Hehea, one of the most ancient kachinas, appears in several ceremonials.

Again, those who had "remembered" were saved, and taken care of by the Ant People. Once they were safe, the twins at the poles were instructed to leave their posts so the world would spin off its axis and out of control. As it traveled through space it froze into solid ice, until the twins took up their stations again and restored the Earth to life, creating a Third World.

Now in the Third World they multiplied in such numbers and advanced so rapidly that they created big cities, countries, a whole civilization. This made it difficult for them to conform to the plan of Creation and to sing praises to Taiowa and Sotuknang. More and more of them became wholly occupied with their own earthly plans.

Some of them, of course, retained the wisdom granted them upon their emergence. With this wisdom they understood that the farther they proceeded on the Road of Life and the more they developed, the harder it was. That was why their world was destroyed every so often to give them a fresh start.

Some Hopi accounts of the Third World contain the tantalizing information that "flying shields" had been developed there, capable of attacking faraway cities and coming back so quickly that no one knew where they had gone. When this world and its advanced civilization was finally destroyed by Sotuknang, this time with great floods, the people who still remembered the plan of Creation took refuge inside the hollow stems of the bamboo. Then came their emergence into the Fourth World.

This time, the people had to search long and hard for a place to establish themselves and start over again. The Hopi tradition tells of endless journeys by boat, paddling uphill all the way. From time to time they would find a place to land, beautiful and bounteous, only to be told by Spider Woman that they must move on: this place was too easy, and soon they would fall into evil ways if they stayed.

Finally, completely exhausted from their fruitless efforts, the people "opened their doors" and let themselves be guided. The water carried them gently to a sandy shore,

Above: A Telavai, or "dawn" kachina, who distributes bean sprouts to all members of a Hopi pueblo during the Powamu Ceremony.
Opposite background and following page 36: Clan markings at Petroglyph National Monument.

where they were greeted by Sotuknang and given further instructions. They were to separate into different groups, each heading in different directions, to claim all the land for the Creator. Each group would have to "follow its own star" to a place where the earth met the sea. They would complete such a journey four times in all, to cover all the four directions, before being guided back together again to settle permanently.

The name of this Fourth World is Tuwaqachi, World Complete. You will find out why. It is not all beautiful and easy like the previous ones. It has height and depth, heat and cold, beauty and barrenness; it has everything for you to choose from. What you choose will determine if this time you can carry out the plan of Creation on it or whether it must in time be destroyed too . . . . You will have help from the proper deities, from your good spirits. Just keep your own doors open and always remember what I have told you. This is what I say.

— Sotuknang, to the new inhabitants of the Fourth World of Tuwaqachi

The Migrations

Most anthropologists assert that the Hopis came to the North American continent as part of the great Mongolian migrations across the Bering Strait, and arrived in the Southwest around 700 A.D. The Hopis' own story is quite different — in fact many traditional narratives speak of the "Back Door" in the north as a place

forbidden to them, where any people who entered did so without permission. In any case, the historical reality is lost in time, and although fragments of it continue to surface—often shattering the suppositions of previous times—it is a story that will perhaps never be fully known.

As the Hopis tell it, however, their history is a rich tapestry of pilgrimage woven in the patterns of the plan set out for them by the Creator. Their accounts of the details are many, varied, and often contradictory. The people who eventually settled together in their desert mesa homeland had spent generations of time apart, formed into their different clans, developing their own traditions and ceremonies. But throughout their journeys they left signs of their passage, and these signs reveal the common threads that bound them even as they went their separate ways.

Modern-day Hopis can readily identify markings that represent the passage of their own clans through places as distant from one another as Ohio and the South American Andes. They can determine, by looking at the symbols, how many of the four rounds of their pilgrimage the clan had completed at the time, in what direction they were moving, and in some cases how long they stayed in this particular place. The implication—that the Hopi migration stories are not only spiritual allegories but also an oral history of actual events in time—is one of the most fascinating and profound aspects of the wisdom carried by the Hopis.

Before the newcomers to the Fourth World set out on their migrations, they were given a tablet (or several tablets—traditional teachings vary, as do accounts of their existence today) containing symbolic representations of their journey and final resting place, and events that would confirm their adherence to the Creator's plan. The tablet best known today is reportedly held by members of the Fire Clan in the present-day village of Hotevilla. This tablet has always had one corner missing that, according to legend, is in possession of a "lost white brother" called Pahana. Pahana's return with the missing corner will signal the beginning of a new brotherhood of mankind.

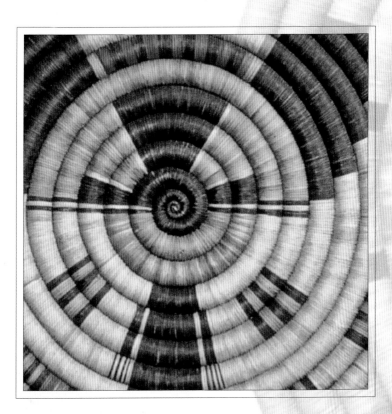

Hopi Social and Spiritual Life

The Clans

The clan affiliations that developed during the period of the Hopi migrations, and which many say existed in the previous worlds also, are central to the Hopi way of life today. One's membership in a particular clan is determined by matrilineal descent, and members of the same or closely related clans are forbidden to intermarry. The names of the clans derive from elements of the natural world—animals, birds, wind, rain, and so on—and each clan carries the knowledge of special powers belonging to the element whose name they carry and the rituals that invoke those powers.

There are four clans who carry out essential functions in relation to ceremonials held throughout the year, and without whom these ceremonials cannot be conducted. Each of these four clans

Above and previous page: Basketry, in the form of decorated plaques and containers, features in Hopi women's ceremonials. *Opposite:* The Soyal Kachina, first to appear in the ceremonial cycle.

also represents one of the four directions. It is said that these are the actual directions from where these clans originally came to settle in the village of Oraibi, long held to be the central, spiritual heart of the Hopi homeland.

Traditionally, the Village Chief of Oraibi has been a member of the Bear Clan. It is generally agreed that the Bear Clan was the first to complete the cycle of four migrations and settle in Oraibi, and many traditional narratives tell of their central role in determining which of the clans that came later would be allowed to stay and under what conditions. It is said that the Bear Clan arrived from the west, and when the four cardinal points are represented in the sacred ceremonies it is always a member of the Bear Clan who takes up the western position.

The "mother" of Oraibi is represented by the Parrot Clan, and a member of this clan represents the southern position in the sacred ceremonies.

This honor was earned, according to tradition, as a result of a long-ago, tragic sacrifice of two children, a Bear Clan boy and a Parrot Clan girl. They had to be sacrificed to a powerful snake-like demon who emerged from the earth in an erupting column of water, threatening the people with destruction.

The other two points of the compass in the sacred ceremonies are represented by the Badger and Eagle clans, occupying north and east respectively. The Badger Clan holds special knowledge of the powers of the spruce tree, whose upturned branches provide a "throne" for the clouds and attract the precious rain. The Eagle Clan contributes feathers for the paho, which carries the remembrances and prayers of

the people to their spiritual father, the sun.

There are many clans in addition to these four, but the Bear, Parrot, Badger, and Eagle are generally acknowledged to be the "leading clans" in the ceremonial religious life of the Hopis. Still, all the other clans have an integral part to play. Their roles in Hopi ceremonies are always related to the powers vested in them as they started their journeys through the Fourth World, and reflect how they have used those powers to benefit the unfoldment of the Creator's plan.

Previous page: Painting of the Hopi Snake Dance. *Left:* The Crow Mother, who arrives in response to an urgent call still dressed in her wedding clothes. *Right:* A kachina representing the mountain sheep.

The Kiva Societies

The kiva now serves as the "temple" of Hopi spiritual life and ceremony, but it has a long history. In the earliest times it was the Hopi dwelling—a small pit dug into the ground and covered with brush and mud. Over time, more sophisticated homes were developed but the kiva structure remained, serving to store food and bury the dead. Jesse Walter Fewkes, an ethnologist who was allowed to live with the Hopis and observe their ceremonials in the late 1800s, believes that in earlier times the sacred ceremonies took place in the homes of the oldest women of the clans. At the time of his study, the Flute Clan conducted its ceremonies in this "ancestral chamber" and traditional narratives indicated that it had always done so.

Nowadays the kivas are the structures used exclusively for ceremonial rites, for gatherings of the kiva society members, and as centers for the initiation of children and young people into the spiritual teachings. The kiva is where the "mouth to ear" transmission of Hopi wisdom takes place, and all activities that happen in this sacred underground chamber are governed by the laws of the Creator.

Traditionally, it is only through initiation into one of the kiva societies that a Hopi can begin to truly understand the complex set of relationships and responsibilities that go into fulfilling the Creator's plan. As Albert Yava puts it, "The individuals who had been initiated into the kiva groups were the 'real' Hopis, and the rest of us were unfulfilled, like unripened corn."

The Annual Ceremonial Cycle

Each year, in correspondence with the movements of the seasons, the sun, the stars, and the moon, the Hopis conduct a series of ceremonial rites to give physical expression to the wisdom that lies at the heart of their Creator's plan. The success of these ceremonies is measured by their results—the coming of rains, the successful harvests, and the harmonious quality of community life. The timing of the ceremonials corresponds to the change of seasons and to the harvests of crops. Some take place exclusively inside the kiva societies, while others involve public performances and dances. The colorful Kachinas, who are spirits of the other world inhabiting human form, arrive to take part in the ceremonials at the beginning of the growing season, and depart again after the last harvests to their place in the other world.

Right: Hopi elders watch the position of the sun to determine the right time for ceremonials.

Waiting

for

Pahana

The tablet given to the Fire Clan at the dawn of the Fourth World is still missing its corner. And with very few exceptions, it could easily be said that the white men who have come to the Hopis have come not to complete this ancient prophecy of a new brotherhood of mankind but to destroy its very possibility.

The first to come were representatives of the Spanish church, who in the seventeenth century used the Hopis as forced labor to build their mission in Oraibi, and to carry out numerous special "personal favors" to their priests. As part of their efforts to convert the local populace the priests would often administer beatings to the "sacrilegious," the "idolatrous," and the "insubordinate." The historic Pueblo Revolt that finally erupted as a result of this brutality is one of the few times the Hopi People of Peace have been known to resort to force. They joined with villages all over the area in August of 1680, in a coordinated effort to drive out the priests and dismantle their churches, stone by stone.

This was not the end of the story, however. The Spanish returned, in time, and were followed much later by other missionaries, other settlers of the "new land" being

Previous page: A jar portraying one of the Hopi deities. *Right:* Leñya, an important kachina in the Flute ceremony.

occupied in ever greater numbers by the European immigrants now flooding North America from east to west. To most of these changes the Hopis responded with characteristic grace and acceptance. But the incursions of the whites, their churches, and their governments, inevitably had profound effects on Hopi life.

Perhaps the most profound disruption of all came in the early twentieth century, with the U.S. government's determined program to educate Native American children in the ways of white society. This program was often carried out by force, against the wishes of the children's parents, and it often caused deep divisions within the communities themselves. Every individual, family, and clan was faced with the conflict between the desire to preserve their sacred traditions and the necessity of dealing with the harsh new realities of the white man's world.

Children were removed from the social and spiritual life of their communities for months and even years at a time. They were dressed in the white man's clothes, had their hair cut in the white man's style, were taught his language, and even given his names. The delicate thread of "mouth to ear" teachings which had survived for

Left: A painting showing marionettes of Corn Maidens who were featured in Hopi ceremonials in the early twentieth century.

centuries was weakened, and even broken in many places. The Hopis, even on their high desert mesa homeland, were not immune from this catastrophic disruption in the continuity of their Road of Life.

Albert Yava, whose Hopi name means "Big Falling Snow," died in 1980. He had grown up in a generation whose lives spanned the great gap between past and future. As a child he was sent to school and for a time enthusiastically adopted the white man's ways. He watched the Christian missionaries come and go, and watched many of his friends convert to Christian beliefs. It was only through a series of fortunate circumstances that he was initiated into his father's kiva society and thereby pulled back to his spiritual roots. It seems fitting, at the end of this brief glimpse into the wisdom of his father's people, to point with his words to the pro-

Above: A doll portraying the Eagle kachina.

found reverence for life that underlies it:

We old-timers can see that there has been a steady drift away from our traditional attitude toward nature and the universe. What I'm talking about is not the dancing and the kiva paraphernalia, all those visible things. They are only a means of expressing what we feel about the world. I am talking about the feelings and the attitudes behind the kiva rituals.

We feel that the world is good. We are grateful to be alive. We are conscious that all men are brothers. We sense that we are related to other living creatures. Life is to be valued and preserved. If you see a grain of corn on the ground, pick it up and take care of it, because it has life inside. When you go out of your house in the morning and see the sun rising, pause a moment to think about it. That sun brings warmth to the things that grow in the fields. If there's a cloud in the sky, look at it and remember that it brings rain to a dry land. When you take water from a spring, be aware that it is a gift of nature.

. . . If you meet a person, you greet him. If he is a stranger or someone you know it is all the same. If someone comes to the village from another place, even if he belongs to a different tribe, feed him. Keep your mind cleansed of evil thoughts against people . . . . Be generous with whatever you have. Avoid injuring others. Respect older people—no matter how they appear to you, they have had hard experiences and have acquired knowledge from living . . . .

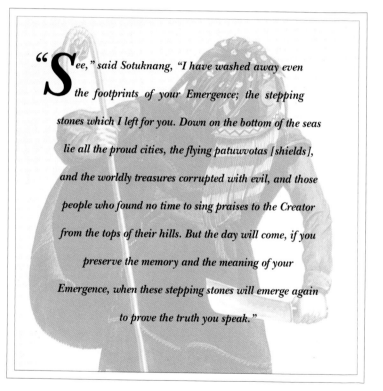

"*See," said Sotuknang, "I have washed away even the footprints of your Emergence; the stepping stones which I left for you. Down on the bottom of the seas lie all the proud cities, the flying patuwvotas [shields], and the worldly treasures corrupted with evil, and those people who found no time to sing praises to the Creator from the tops of their hills. But the day will come, if you preserve the memory and the meaning of your Emergence, when these stepping stones will emerge again to prove the truth you speak.*"

It is this simple thread that the Hopi people have managed to hold on to for centuries, in all its joy and life, its sound and color. The fact that it has survived a generation of cataclysmic change recalls other words, spoken in a different time, that must have also seemed cataclysmic to those who were there:

"See," said Sotuknang, "I have washed away even the footprints of your Emergence; the stepping-stones which I left for you. Down on the bottom of the seas lie all the proud cities, the flying patuwvotas [shields], and the worldly treasures corrupted with evil, and those people who found no time to sing praises to the Creator from the tops of their hills. But the day will come, if you preserve the memory and the meaning of your Emergence, when these stepping-stones will emerge again to prove the truth you speak."

These words were spoken by Sotuknang at the beginning of the Fourth World, and they still ring with a promise of what is to come. Now, as the twentieth century draws to a close, it is said that the young people of the Hopis are showing a renewed interest in the teachings of the elders. The thread of Hopi wisdom may yet survive to see the fulfillment of its prophecy of a new brotherhood of mankind.

Left background: Soyoko, an important figure in the purification rites of Powamu. *Following page:* Ahaliya, the "uncle" of all the kachinas.

Fewkes, Jesse Walter. *Archeological Expedition to Arizona in 1895;* 17th Annual Report of the Bureau of American Ethnology (1895-96), Washington, D.C., 1898.

—— *Hopi Katchinas Drawn by Native Artists;* Twenty-first Annual Report of the Bureau of American Ethnology (1899-1900), Washington D.C., 1903.

Voth, H.R. *The Traditions of the Hopi,* Field Columbian Museum Publication 96. Chicago, 1905.

Walters, Frank, and Oswald White Bear Fredericks. *Book of the Hopi.* Viking Penguin, New York, 1977.

Yava, Albert. *Big Falling Snow: A Tewa-Hopi Indian's Life and Times and the History and Traditions of His People.* Edited and Annotated by Harold Courlander. University of New Mexico Press, Albuquerque, 1992.

Docstader, Frederick J. *The Kachina and the White Man: A Study of the Influence of White Culture on the Hopi Kachina Cult.* Cranbrook Institute of Science, Bulletin 35. Bloomfield Hills, Michigan, 1934.

Malotki, Ekkehart and Michael Lomatuway'ma. *Hopi Coyote Tales: Istutuwutsi.* Lincoln: University of Nebraska Press, 1984.

Nequatewa, Edmund. *Truth of a Hopi and Other Clan Stories of Shung-opovi.* Museum of Northern Arizona, Bulletin No. 8. Flagstaff, Arizona, 1946.

Simmons, Leo W. (ed.). *Sun Chief, The Autobiography of a Hopi Indian.* New Haven, Conn.: Yale University Press for the Institute of Human Relations, 1942.

Thompson, Laura. *Culture in Crisis: A Study of the Hopi Indians.* New York: Harper, 1950.

Titiev, Mischa. *Old Oraibi: A Study of the Hopi Indians of Third Mesa.* Papers of the Peabody Museum of American Archaeology and Ethnology, Vol. 22, No. 1. Cambridge, Mass. 1944.

Every effort has been made to trace all present copyright holders of the material used in this book, whether companies or individuals. Any omission is unintentional, and we will be pleased to correct errors in future editions of this book.

Text acknowledgments:

pp. 20, 22, 23, 26, 33, 35, 56, 57, back cover: From *Book of the Hopi* by Frank Waters. Copyright © 1963 by Frank Waters. Used by permission of Viking Penguin, a division of Penguin Books USA Inc.

pp. 17, 55: From *Big Falling Snow – A Tewa-Hopi Indian's Life and Times and the History and Traditions of His People,* by Albert Yava, edited and annotated by Harold Courlander, University of New Mexico Press, Albuquerque, New Mexico, 1982. Originally published by Crown Publishers, New York, 1978. Copyright © 1978 by Harold Courlander.

Special thanks go to Terry P. Wilson, Professor of Native American Studies at the University of California, Berkeley. His help in checking the accuracy of information and the sensitivity of the language used in this work has been invaluable.

Picture acknowledgments:

Detta B. Lange; Page: 12.
Museum of New Mexico, H. F. Robinson; Page 7.
Museum of Northern Arizona; Page: 14.
Jesse Walter Fewkes, 'Hopi Kachinas'; Pages: 51, 52.
Reproduced by permission of the National Museum of the American Indian, Smithsonian Institution;. Pages: 4, 8, 10, 16, 18, 20, 25, 27, 28, 30, 31, 32, 34, 38, 40, 41, 42, 44, 45, 47, 48, 54, 56, 58, cover.